P9-CAM-726

GIFTED & TALENTED®

*To develop
your child's gifts
and talents*

GIFTED & TALENTED®

*To develop
your child's gifts
and talents*

A Workbook for Ages 4–6

Written by Cookie Spancer • Illustrated by Leesa Whitten

Lowell 🏠 House
Juvenile
Los Angeles
CONTEMPORARY
BOOKS
Chicago

ISBN 0-929923-82-0

10 9

Cover design: Brenda Leach
Cover illustration: Dave Lowe

Note to Parents

GIFTED AND TALENTED WORKBOOKS will help develop your child's natural talents and gifts by providing activities to enhance critical and creative thinking skills. These skills of logic and reasoning teach children **how** to think. They are precisely the skills emphasized by teachers of gifted and talented children.

Thinking skills are the skills needed to be able to learn anything at any time. Unlike events, words, and teaching methods, thinking skills never change. If a child has a grasp of how to think, school success and even success in life will become more assured. In addition, the child will become self-confident as he or she approaches new tasks with the ability to think them through and discover solutions.

GIFTED AND TALENTED WORKBOOKS present these skills in a unique way, combining the basic subject areas of reading, language arts, and math with thinking skills. The top of each page is labeled to indicate the specific thinking skill developed. Here are some of the skills you will find:

- Deduction – the ability to reach a logical conclusion by interpreting clues

- Understanding Relationships – the ability to recognize how objects, shapes, and words are similar or dissimilar; to classify and categorize

- Sequencing – the ability to organize events, numbers; to recognize patterns

- Inference – the ability to reach logical conclusions from given or assumed evidence

- Creative Thinking – the ability to generate unique ideas; to compare and contrast the same elements in different situations; to present imaginative solutions to problems

How to Use Gifted & Talented Workbooks

Each book contains activities that challenge children. The activities vary in range from easier to more difficult. You may need to work with your child on many of the pages, especially with the child who is a non-reader. However, even a non-reader can master thinking skills, and the sooner your child learns how to think, the better. Read the directions to your child, and if necessary, explain them. Let your child choose to do the activities that interest him or her. When interest wanes, stop. A page or two at a time may be enough, as the child should have fun while learning.

It is important to remember that these activities are designed to teach your child **how to think,** not how to find the right answer. Teachers of gifted children are never surprised when a child discovers a new "right" answer. For example, a child may be asked to choose the object that doesn't belong in this group: a table, a chair, a book, a desk. The best answer is **book,** since all the others are furniture. But a child could respond that all of them belong because they all could be found in an office. The best way to react to this type of response is to praise the child and gently point out that there is another answer too. While creativity should be encouraged, your child must look for the best and most **suitable** answer.

GIFTED AND TALENTED WORKBOOKS have been written and designed by teachers. Educationally sound and endorsed by leaders in the gifted field, this series will benefit any child who demonstrates curiosity, imagination, a sense of fun and wonder about the world, and a desire to learn. These books will open your child's mind to new experiences and help fulfill his or her true potential.

Which cookie goes in each bag? Draw a line from each cookie to the bag it matches.

Which toy goes in each bag? Draw a line from each toy to the bag it matches.

Which box has all the robot's pieces? Draw a line from the robot to the box that has all the pieces.

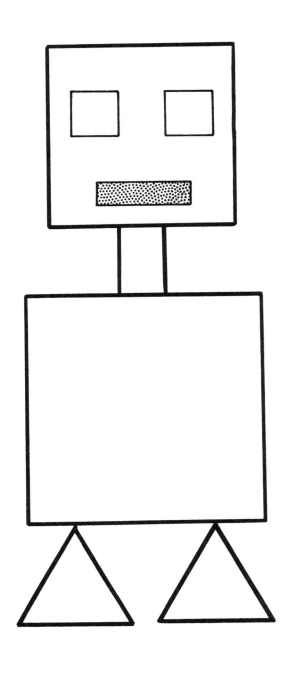

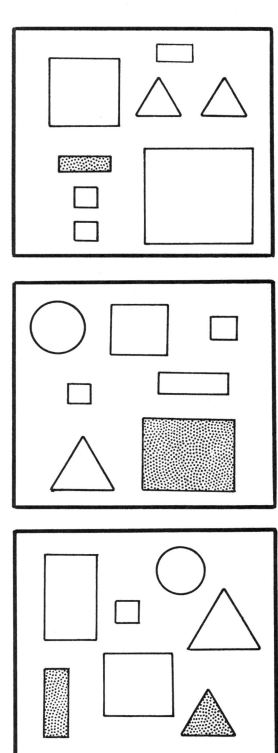

Which box has all the doll's clothes? Draw a line from the doll to the box that has the same clothes she is wearing.

Which blocks did Ann use to make her tower?
Draw a line from the tower to the box that has
all the blocks she used.

Use these shapes to draw a toy: ◯ △ ▢ ▭ .You can use the shapes as many times as you like.

MY TOY

All of these are **Roops**:

They are all Roops because they all have **dots**.

None of these are Roops:

They are **not** Roops because they do **not** have dots.

Draw a line under each Roop.

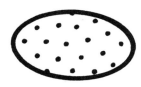   

Draw your own Roop here:

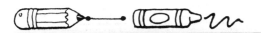

All of these are **Zipps**:

  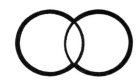

They are all Zipps because they are all made with **circles.**

None of these are Zipps:

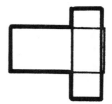   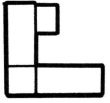

They are **not** Zipps because they are **not** made with circles.

Draw a line under each Zipp.

  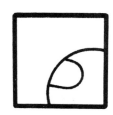  

Draw your own Zipp here:

All of these are **Neeps**:

None of these are Neeps:

Draw a line under the Neeps.

 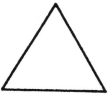 

Make your own Neep here:

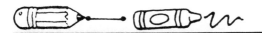

All of these are **Sloobs:**

None of these are Sloobs:

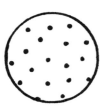   

Draw a line under the Sloobs.

Make your own Sloob here:

All of these are **Marps:**

None of these are Marps:

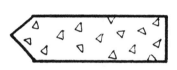   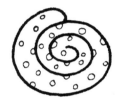

Draw a line under the Marps.

 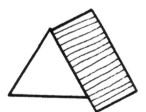  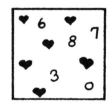

Make your own Marp here:

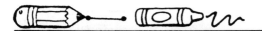

Now make up your own. What do you think a **Gugie** would look like? What makes all **Gugies** look the same?

_____

All of these are **Gugies:**

_____

None of these are Gugies:

_____

Draw one big Gugie here:

_____

What comes next? Draw the picture that comes next in each row.

    _____

X X ◯ X X _____

    _____

    _____

◯ ◯ X ◯ ◯ _____

    _____

  _____

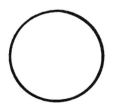   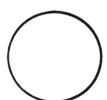 _____

Draw the missing parts of the pattern on the flag. Color the flag.

Draw the missing beads to finish the pattern on the necklace.

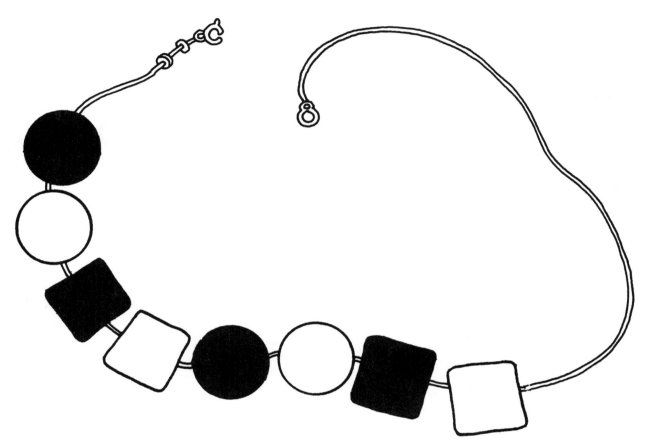

Make a bracelet to match!

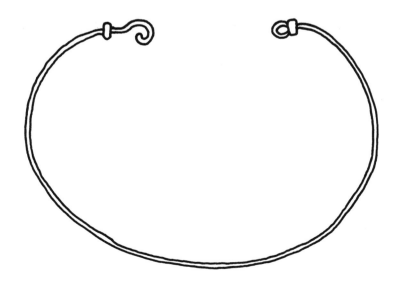

Color the ✿ purple.

Color the 🐟 green.

Make a new pattern by using **different** colors!

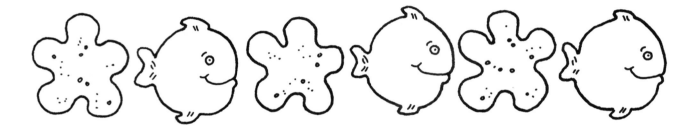

Make another new pattern with colors.

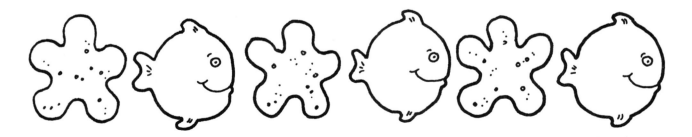

Design your own wrapping paper! Draw your pattern on the wrapping paper below.

Draw a line from each pair of boots to its matching umbrella.

Color each rain hat so that there is one hat to match each set of umbrellas and boots.

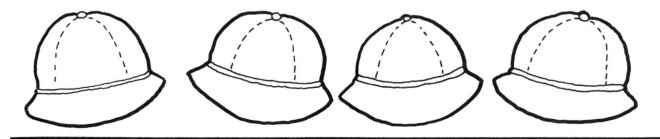

Draw a line from each headband to the belt that it matches.

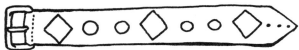

Draw a headband with your own pattern.

Draw the rest of this clown. Be sure to give him all his missing parts!

These things have been cut in half! Draw the halves that are missing.

Draw a line to the missing picture. The first one has been done for you.

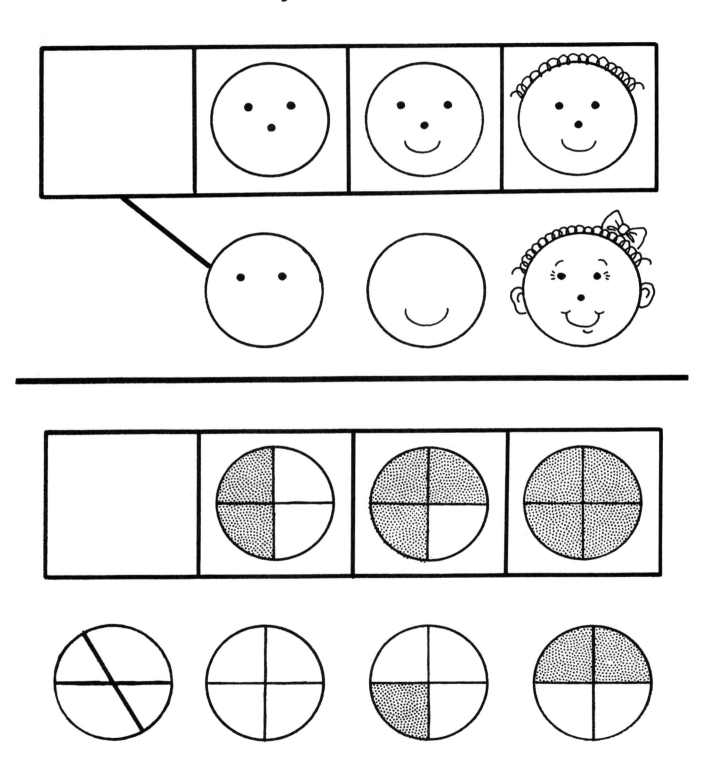

Draw a line to the missing picture.

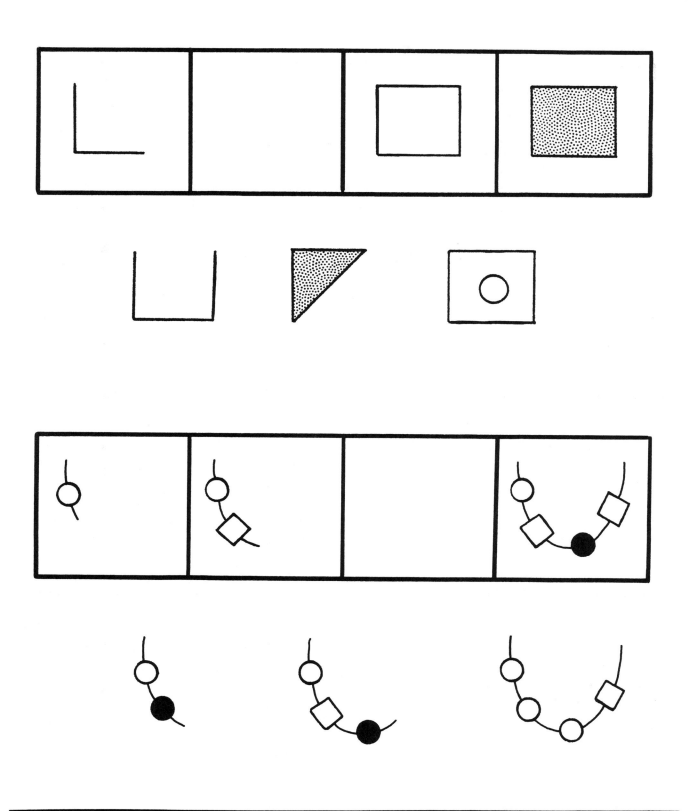

Draw a line to the missing picture.

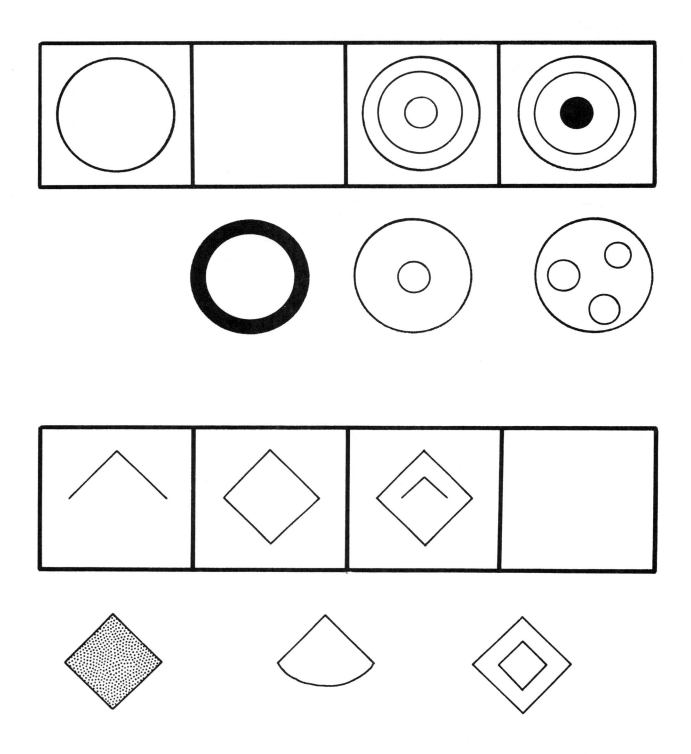

Connect the dots with straight lines to draw as **many** squares as you can.
Make them in different sizes!
Two have been done for you.

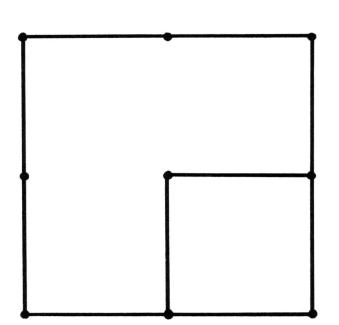

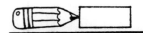

Connect the dots to draw as **many** rectangles as you can. Make them in different sizes! Two have been done for you.

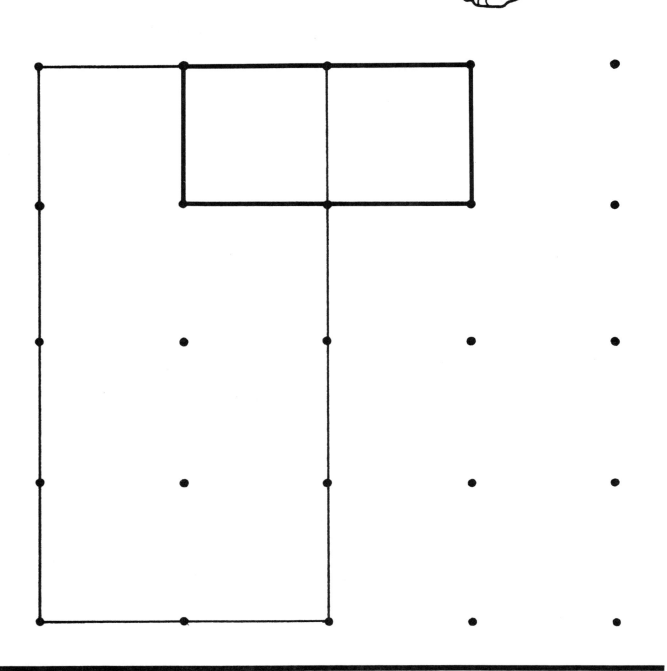

Connect the dots and draw as many triangles as you can. Don't forget to use different sizes!

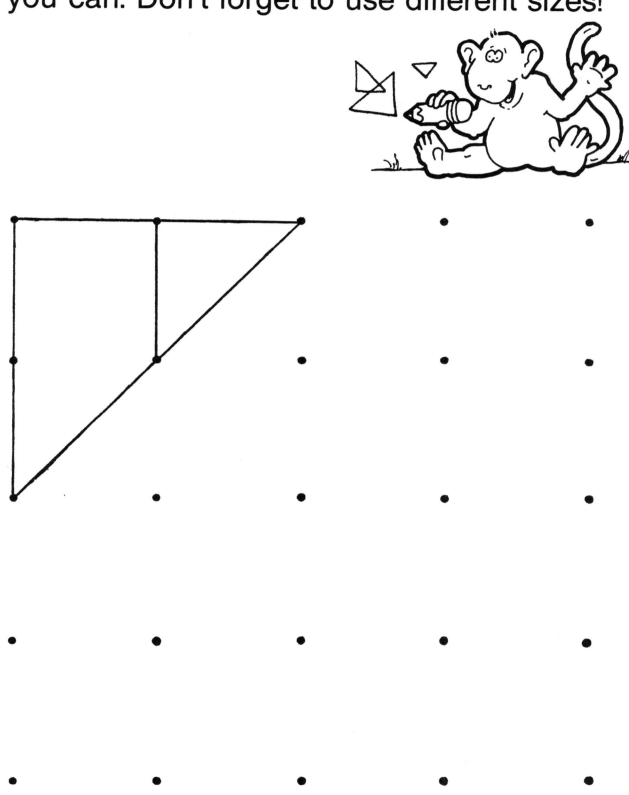

Trace the shapes below.

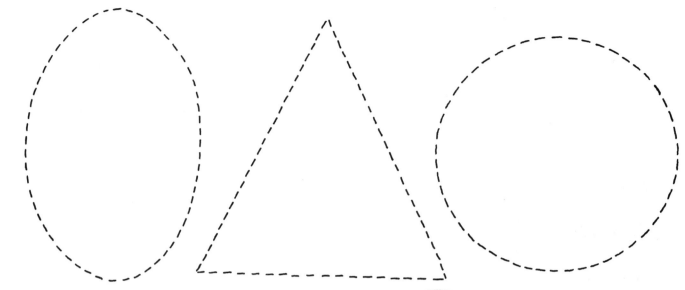

Fill in the face. The eyes are ◯ 's . The nose is a △ . The mouth is a ◯ .

Trace the shapes below.

Color the ☐ 's blue.

Color the ▭ 's green.

Color the △ 's red.

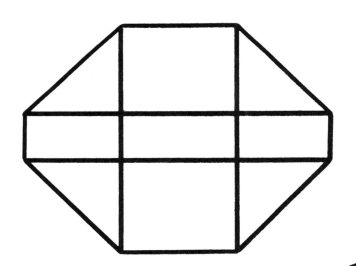

How many ☐ 's? _____

How many ▭ 's? _____

How many △ 's? _____

Circle the number of 's you see in each design.

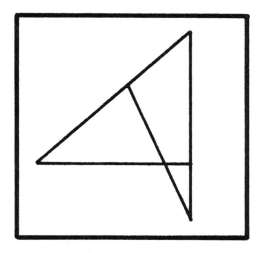

2   3   4   5

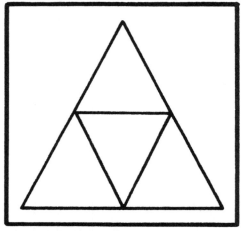

3   4   5   6

6 7 8 9

Make your own design by using **only** ▭ 's, ▽ 's, and □ 's.

How many ▭ 's? _____

How many ▽ 's? _____

How many □ 's? _____

A **pentagon** has **five** sides and **five** corners.
Trace the pentagons:

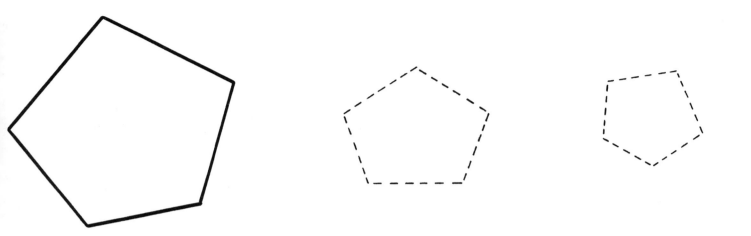

Color the biggest one purple.
Color the smallest one orange.

Draw the lines you need to finish the pentagon.

Can you make it look like a birdhouse?

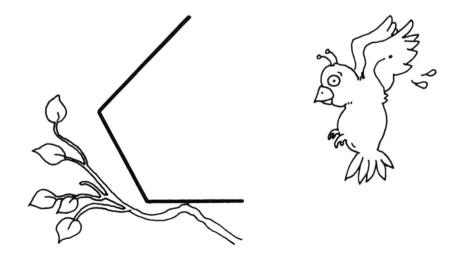

A pentagon has five sides and five corners.

Find the **three** pentagons below and color them.

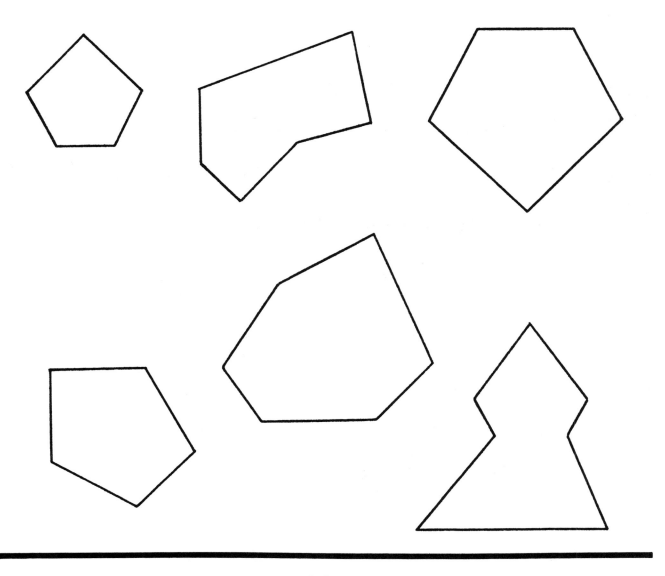

A **hexagon** has **six** sides and **six** corners.

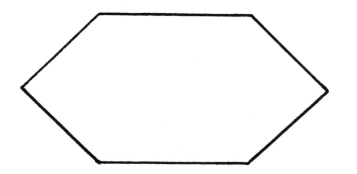

Trace the hexagons.

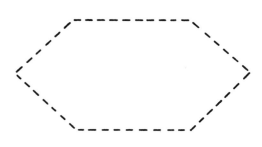
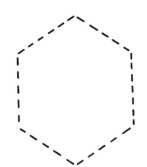
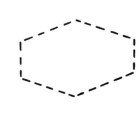

Color the biggest one blue.
Color the smallest one red.
Draw the lines you need to finish the hexagon.
Then make it look like a sign by writing your name inside!

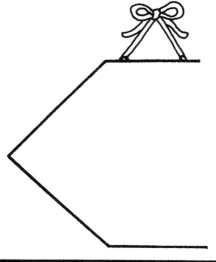

A hexagon has six sides and six corners.

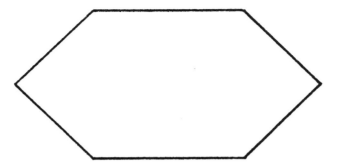

Find the **three** hexagons below and color them.

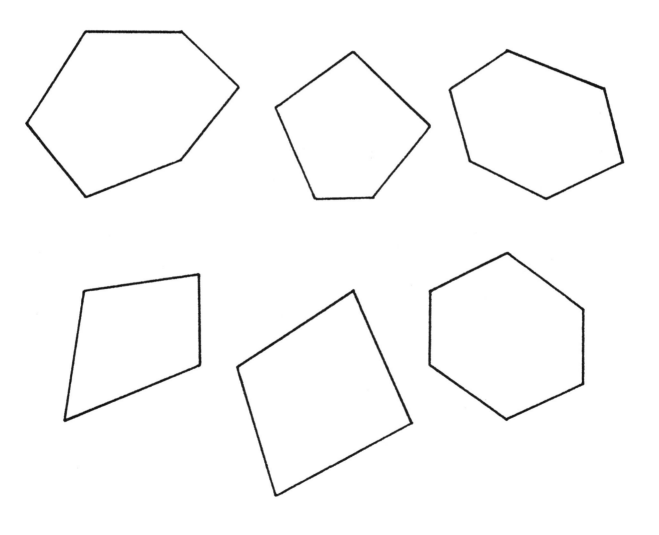

An **octagon** has **eight** sides and **eight** corners.

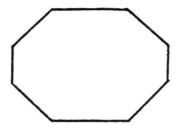

Trace the octagons.

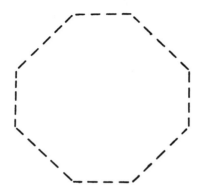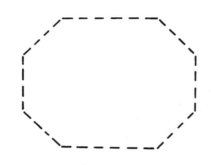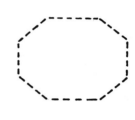

Color the biggest one red.
Color the smallest one yellow.

A STOP sign is an octagon. Draw the lines you need to finish the STOP sign. Color it red.

An octagon has eight sides and eight corners.

Find the **two** octagons below and color them.

Color the shapes: Circles ◯ — green.

Pentagons ⬠ — orange.

Rectangles ▭ — purple.

Hexagons ⬡ — yellow.

Octagons ⬢ — red.

Count
the shapes:

Circles ◯ __ Pentagons ⬠ __ Rectangles ▭ __

Hexagons ⬡ __ Octagons ⬢ __

Which Jack-O-Lantern belongs to Mike? Read all about Mike's Jack-O-Lantern. Then color it.

The mouth is a triangle △.

The nose is round.

The eyes are the same shape as its mouth.

Which design is Mary's? Read all about Mary's design. Then color it.

It has one circle ○.

It has four triangles △.

It does **not** have any squares □.

It has three rectangles ▭.

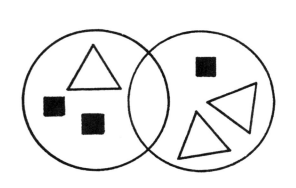

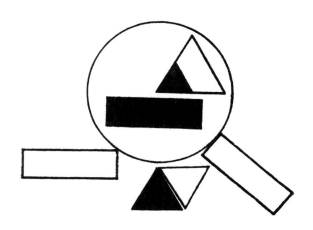

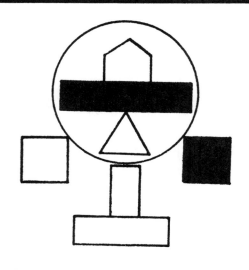

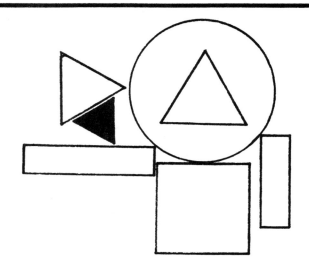

Which house is David's house? Read all about David's house. Then color it.

The windows are octagons .

The roof is a triangle △.

There is a pentagon ⬠ on the roof!

The door is a rectangle ▭.

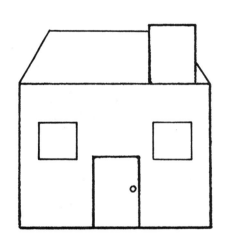

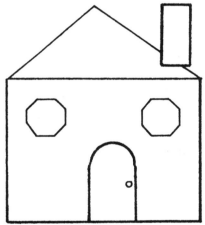

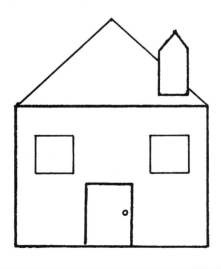

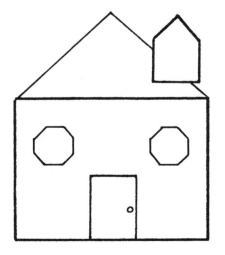

Which picture did the cat paint? Read all about the cat's picture. Then color it.

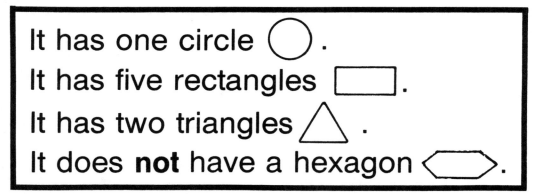

It has one circle ⬭.
It has five rectangles ▭.
It has two triangles △.
It does **not** have a hexagon ⬡.

Which dish of ice cream belongs to Willy? Read all about Willy's ice cream. Then color it.

It has more than two scoops of ice cream.
It has less than five scoops of ice cream.

Which bug did Jon catch? Read all about Jon's bug. Then color it.

It has more than three legs.

It has less than eight legs.

Which monster is on T.V.? Read all about the monster. Then color it.

It has more than two eyes.

It has less than five eyes.

It has more than one nose.

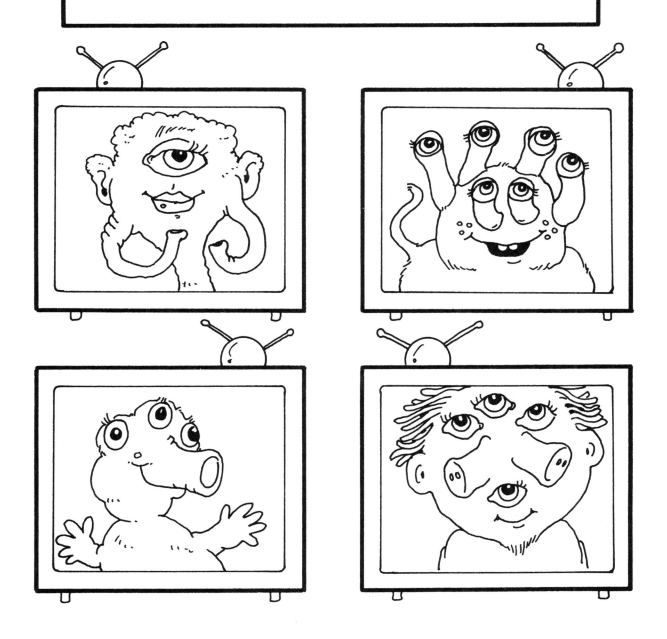

A Curly is any clown that has curly hair.
Here is a Curly:

Put a around all the Curlies.

Put a ◯ around the number of Curlies you found:

0   1   2   3   4

A Smiley is any clown that is smiling.
Here is a Smiley:

Put a △ around all the Smileys.

Put a △ around the number of Smileys you found:

0   1   2   3   4

A Bouncy is any clown holding a ball.
Here is a Bouncy:

Put a ☐ around all the Bouncies.

Put a ☐ around the number of Bouncies you found:

0   1   2   3   4

Put a around all the Curlies 's.

Put a around all the Smileys 's.

Put a around all the Bouncies 's.

The first one has been done for you.

1

2

3

4

Which one is a Curly-Bouncy? ___1___

Which one is a Curly-Smiley? _____

Which one is a Bouncy? _____

Which one is a Smiley-Bouncy? _____

Finish this clown so he will be a Smiley-Curly.

A Yummy is any ice cream treat that has whipped cream.

Here is a Yummy:

Put a  around all the Yummies.

Put a ◯ around the number of Yummies you found.

0   1   2   3   4

A Wowie is any ice cream treat that has only 2 scoops of ice cream.

Here is a Wowie:

Put a △ around all the Wowies.

Put a △ around the number of Wowies you found:

0   1   2   3

A Fruity is any ice cream treat that has cherries.

Here is a Fruity:

Put a ☐ around all the Fruities.

Put a ☐ around the number of Fruities you found:

0   1   2   3   4

Put a around all the Yummies .

Put a △ around all the Wowies  .

Put a ☐ around all the Fruities .

The first one is done for you.

1

2

3

4

Which one is a Yummy-Wowie? _____1_____

Which one is a Wowie-Fruity? _____

Which one is a Fruity? _____

Which one is a Yummy-Fruity? _____

Make your own Yummy-Wowie-Fruity.

A Creepy is any creature with more than two legs.

Here is a Creepy:

Put a ◯ around all the Creepies.

Put a ◯ around the number of Creepies you found.

0   1   2   3   4

A Fuzzy is any creature with hair.

Here is a Fuzzy:

Put a  around all the Fuzzies:

Put a △ around the number of Fuzzies you found.

0   1   2   3   4

A Pointy is any creature that has horns.

Here is a Pointy.

Put a  around all Pointies.

Put a ☐ around the number of Pointies you found.

0   1   2   3   4

Put a ○ around all Creepies .

Put a △ around all Fuzzies .

Put a ☐ around all Pointies .

The first one is done for you.

1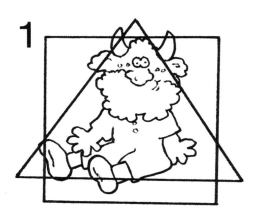

2

3

4

Which one is a Fuzzy-Pointy? _____1_____

Which one is a Creepy-Fuzzy? _____

Which one is a Pointy? _____

Which one is a Fuzzy? _____

Make your own Fuzzy-Creepy-Pointy.

This is the way we count by 2's:

0 ₁ **2** ₃ **4** ₅ **6** ₇ **8** ₉ **10** ₁₁ **12** ₁₃ **14** ₁₅ **16** ₁₇ **18** ₁₉ **20**

Color the balloons as you count by 2's from 0 to 20. Three balloons don't belong!

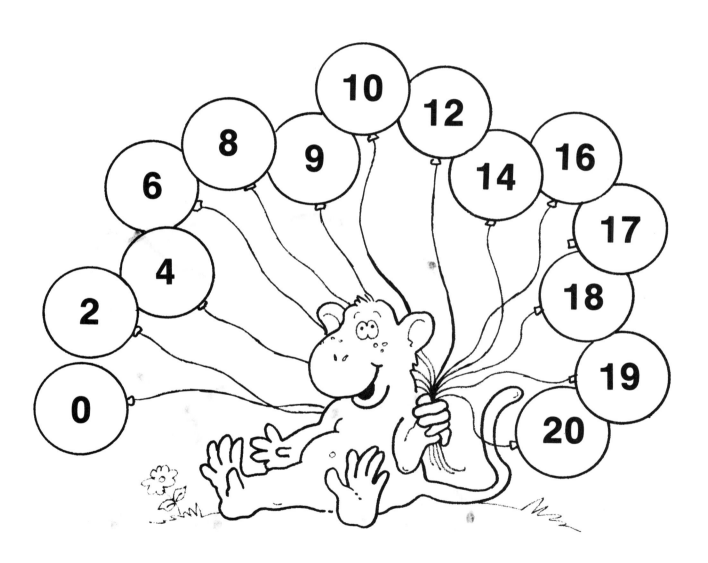

Complete this picture by following the dots as you count by 2's from 0 to 20. The first line has been drawn for you.

This is the way we count by 5's:

0 -1-2-3-4- 5 -6-7-8-9- 10 -11-12-13-14- 15 -16-17-18-19- 20 -21-22-23-24- 25 -26-27-28-29 30 -31-32-33-34- 35 -36-37-38-39- 40 -41-42-43-44- 45 -46-47-48-49- 50

Color all the gifts you need to count by 5's from 0 to 50. Four gifts don't belong!

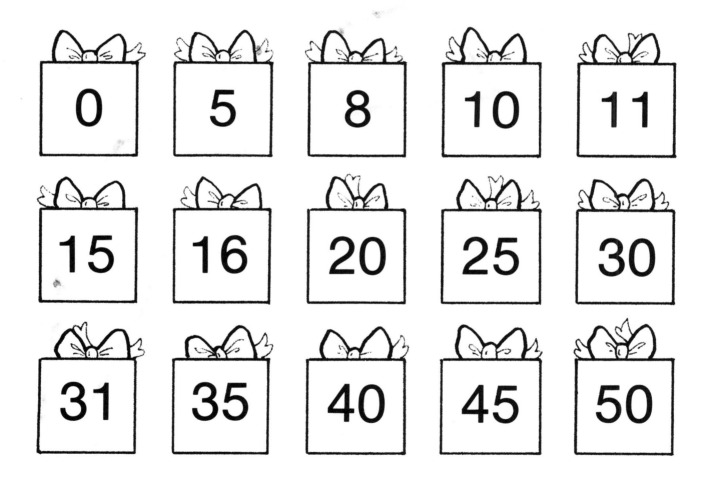

Complete this picture by following the dots as you count by 5's from 0 to 50. The first line has been drawn for you.

This is the way we count by 10's:

0-10-20-30-40-50-60-70-80-90-100

Color the fish you need to count by 10's from 0 to 100. Four fish don't belong!

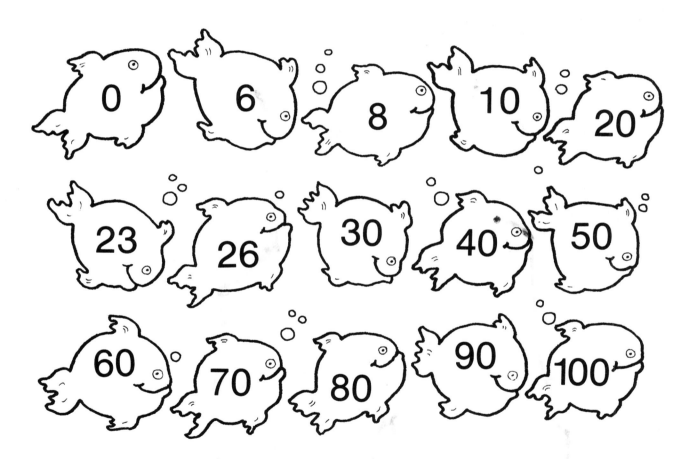

Complete this picture by following the dots as you count by 10's from 0 to 100. The first line has been drawn for you.

This is the way we count by 100's:

0 - 100 - 200 - 300 - 400 - 500 - 600 - 700 - 800 - 900 - 1,000

Color all the turtles you need to count by 100's from 0 to 1,000. Three turtles don't belong!

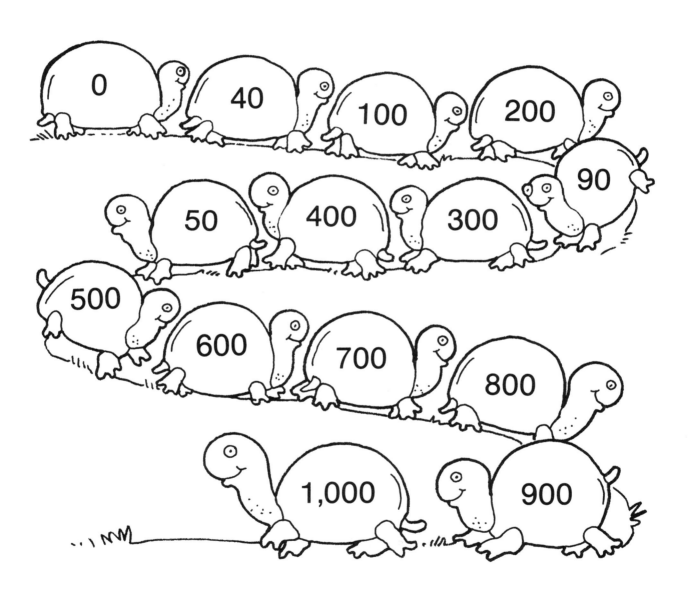

Finish this picture by connecting the dots as you count by 100's from 0 to 1,000.

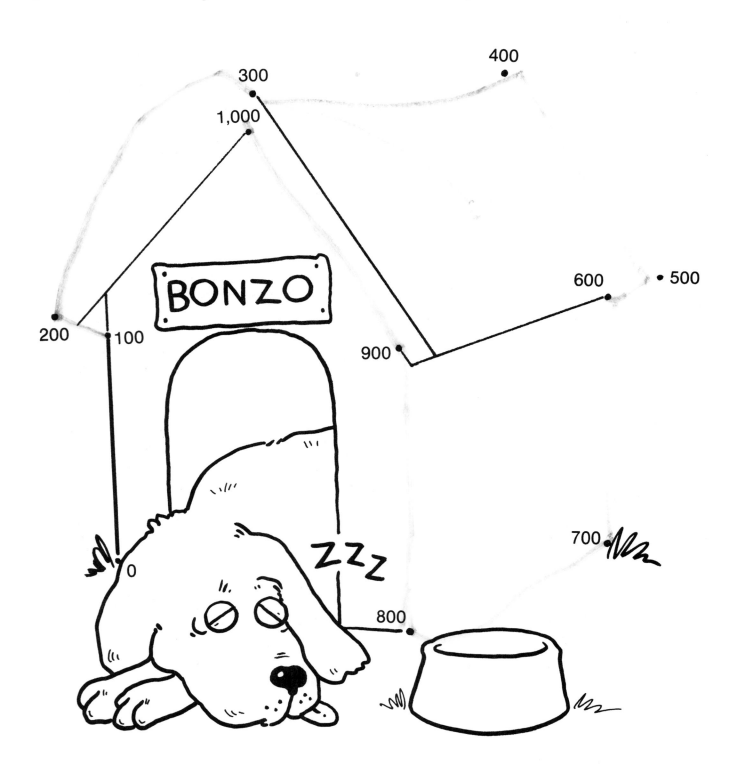

Look at this picture quickly. Then close your eyes and guess how many -shaped cookies are in the jar.

Turn the page to find the answer.

Did you see all these hearts?

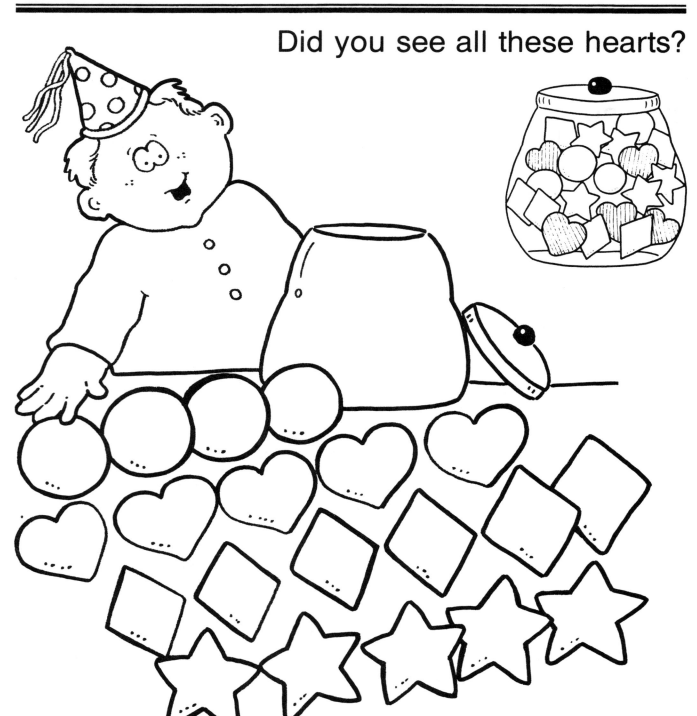

How many ◯'s?_____   How many ♡'s? _____

How many ◇'s? _____   How many ☆'s?_____

Look at this picture quickly. Then close your eyes and guess how many  marbles are in the bag.

Turn the page to find the answer.

Did you see all these  marbles?

Count each set of marbles.

How many 's?____ How many 's?____

How many 's?____ How many 's?____

Look at this picture quickly. Then close your eyes and guess how many bears are in the machine.

Turn the page to find the answer.

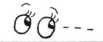

Did you see all these bears?

How many 's? _____ How many _____'s?_____

How many _____'s?_____ How many _____ 's?_____

This graph shows how many animals are at the zoo.

How many 's? **2** How many 's? **2**

How many 's? **0** How many 's? **1**

The children made a garden. This graph shows how many flowers they planted.

How many 's?____ How many 🌹's? ____

How many 🌼's?____ How many 🌸's?____

Note: Point out to your child that some graphs go sideways and some go up and down.

4 children were .

3 children were .

Fill in the graph with pictures.

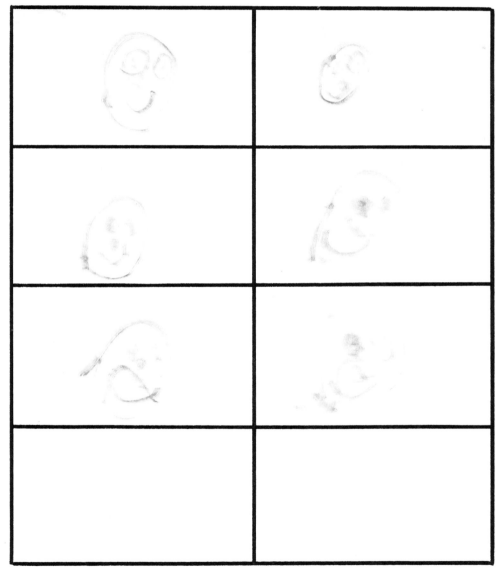

5 days were .

2 days were .

3 days were ⬚ .

Fill in the graph with pictures.

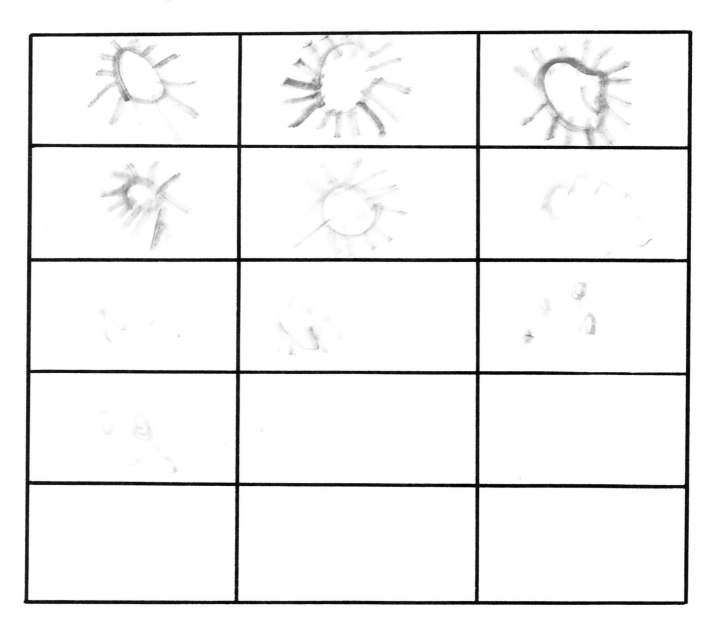

Look at the pictures. Look at the graph below.

There is one ▨ for each toy. How many ⊕ 's
do you see? Color one ☐ for each ⊕ .

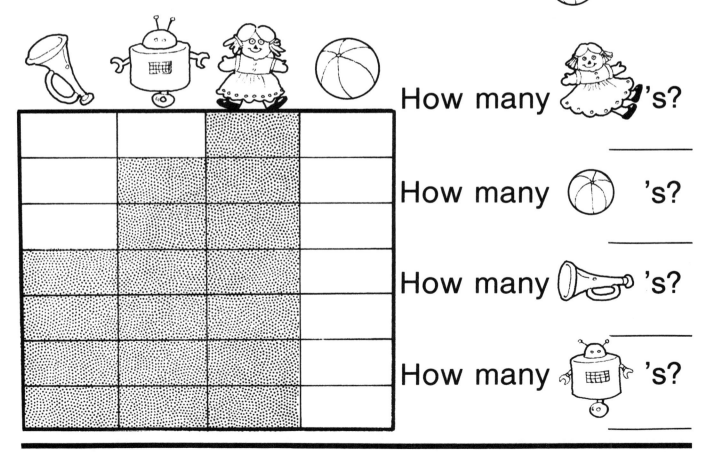

How many 's?____ How many 's?____
How many 's?____ How many 's?____

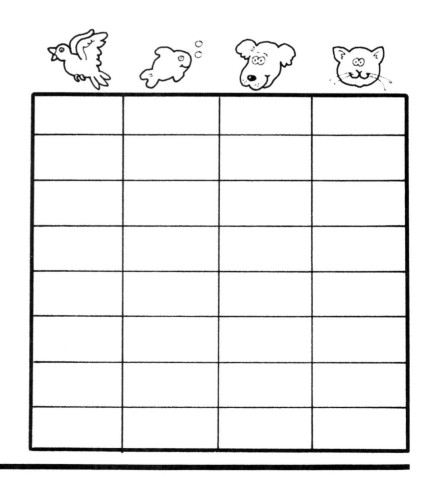

Color in
one [   ]
for each pet.

How many ⊘'s? ____   How many ⎯'s? ____

How many ⊙'s? ____   How many ╱'s? ____

Fill in the ▯'s.

How many winter clothes ? _____

How many summer clothes ? _____

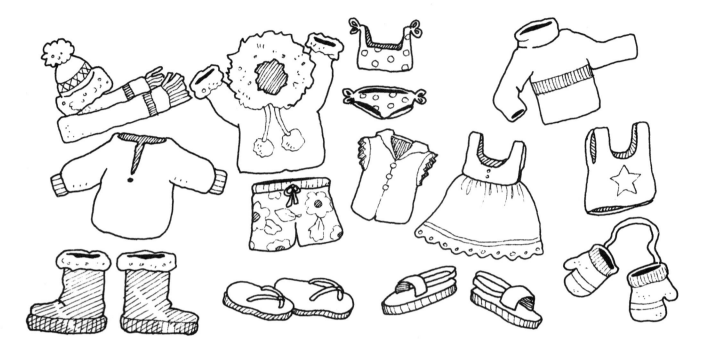

Fill in the ☐'s.

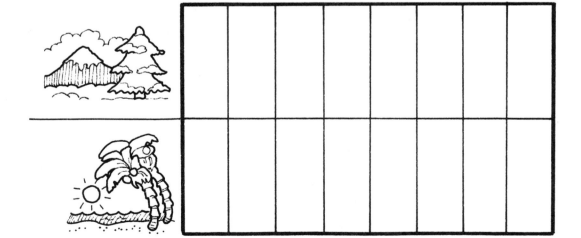

How many things belong in the sky 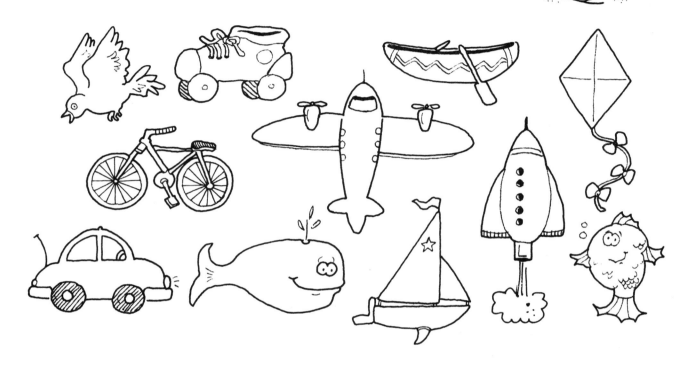 ? ____

How many things belong in the water ? ____

How many things belong on the land ? ____

Fill in the ☐ 's.

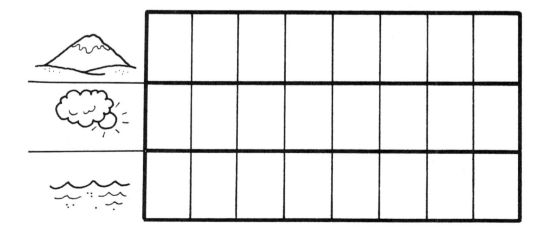

How many things have 1 wheel? _____
How many things have 2 wheels? _____
How many things have 3 wheels? _____
How many things have 4 wheels? _____

Fill in the ☐ 's.

1 wheel	2 wheels	3 wheels	4 wheels

Look at all the shapes, one at a time. When you think you can remember them all, turn to the back of this page.

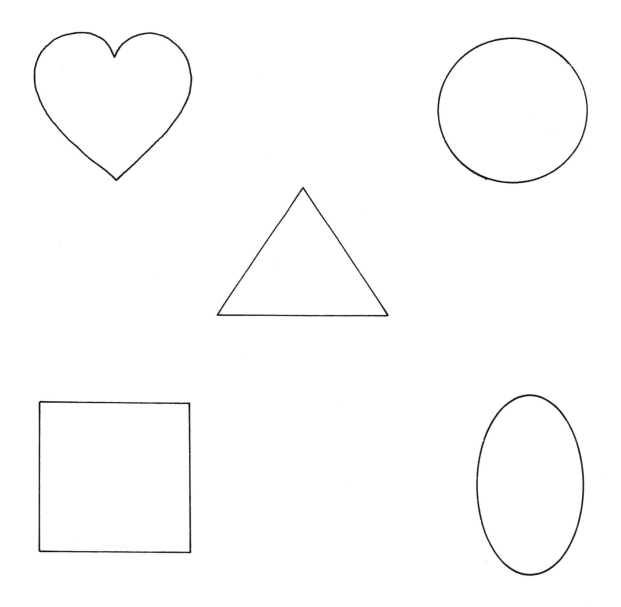

Find the shapes you saw on the page before. Circle only the shapes you saw on the page before.

Now turn back and check. Did you remember them all?

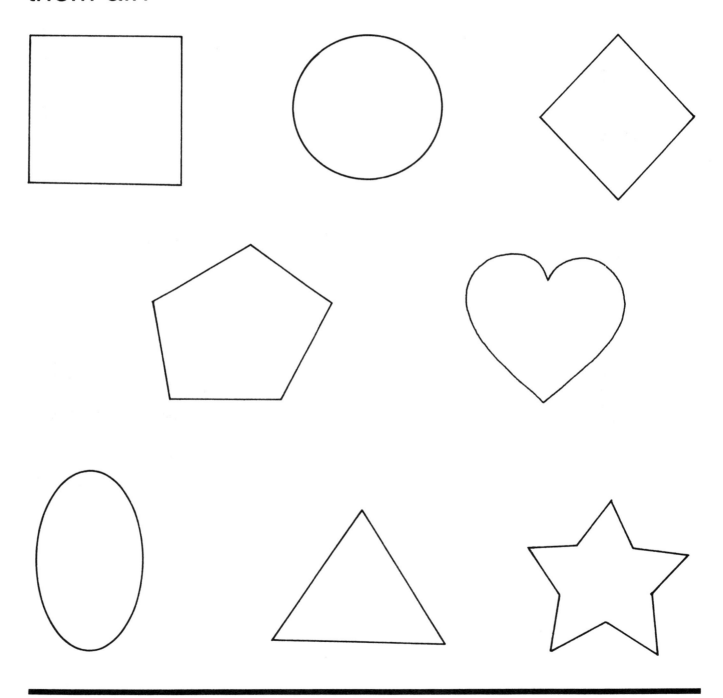

Look at all the numbers, one at a time. When you think you can remember them all, turn to the back of this page.

6   8   10

12   14   16

Find the numbers you saw on the page before.
Circle only the numbers you saw on the
page before.

4   6   10   14

9   16   5   8

22   12

Now turn back and check. Did you remember
them all?

Look at the numbers, one at a time. When you think you can remember them all, turn to the back of this page.

10 15 20

25 30

35 40

Find the numbers you saw on the page before.
Circle only the numbers you saw on the
page before.

10	**12**	**14**	**15**
20	**25**	**45**	**50**
30	**35**	**40**	**5**

Now turn back and check. Did you remember
them all?

MM-EC/1092-7/PB909